JERKY MAKING

—for the home, trail, and campfire

by Brad Prowse

Naturegraph Publishers

Library of Congress Cataloging-in-Publication Data
Prowse, Brad, 1935-
   jerky making / by Brad Prowse ; illus. by Matt Prowse.
      p.   cm.
   ISBN 0-87961-247-9 (alk. paper)
   1. Dried beef. 2. Marinades. I. Title.
TX749.5.B43P76   1997
641.6'62–dc21   97-17016
                                                            CIP

Illustrations by Matt Prowse

Naturegraph Publishers has been publishing books on natural history, Native Americans, and outdoor subjects since 1946. Please write for our free catalog.

Books for a better world

Naturegraph Publishers, Inc.
3543 Indian Creek Road
Happy Camp, CA 96039
USA

Table of Contents

Foreword

I can hear your screams now. "I paid good money for this skinny little book?" But wait! This little book is a compilation of all the things I've learned, through trial and error, about making jerky at home. Read carefully, it should save you a lot of time and money because you won't have to stumble along as I did, learning the hard way all the jerky tips and techniques I list here. The money you save on your first few batches of jerky, and the satisfaction of making it yourself, will more than pay for this book.

Introduction

Jerky was probably humankind's earliest attempt at preserving food. In fact, it might even predate the human invention of it. The first jerky might have been made by some giant creature, a mastodon perhaps, accidentally stepping on some little animal trying to scurry out of the way. (This also may have been the world's first roadkill.) After the crushed critter had baked in the hot sun a few days, maybe Ooog, a prehuman who occupied a nearby cave condo, passed by. Seeing the flattened mess, he may have taken a bite out of it and thought, "Uh! Not bad!"

Whether Ooog got the idea to start drying meat on his own or just hung around the mastodons, hoping for another mashed mammal, we'll never know. But, by the time we come to Homo sapiens, the process of drying meat was probably pretty widespread.

For some of us, the word "jerky" is reminiscent of the American Indians, who taught us how to make jerky. Oddly enough, dried meat doesn't seem to have been used much by the Europeans who colonized the new country. For them, salting meat or pickling it in brine were the normal ways of preservation. This kept the meat closer to its original butchered state than drying does, but it also made it more unwieldy to transport and store. In the Old World, towns, settlements, and permanent farms were the norm. Hence, preserving food by pickling or salting was no problem, as the residents didn't have to toss pickling barrels or slabs of salted beef into wagons and hie themselves to new lands on a regular basis.

In contrast, the buffalo meat and the meat of other animals the Indians dried was lightweight, highly portable, and had a long "shelf life." The Plains Indians were primarily hunter-gatherers. They had to get their food stores in between spring and fall, when plants were growing and the buffalo herds were moving about. After they got the horse, it was also the time of year when their ponies were well fed and ready for the hunt. Since their food had to last them all through the winter and be portable because hunters and gatherers did a lot of moving about, drying was the perfect solution. (The word "jerky" by the way may come from the Spanish word "charqui," which, according to one dictionary I have, means to pull (jerk) or cut into long strips.)

Another point; since the Europeans had domestic animals for meat, going out and knocking ol' bossy in the head and slicing her up was fairly easy, even in winter. There often was no need to keep a large supply of preserved meat on hand. Other than dogs early Native Americans had no domestic animals. Though they did domesticate the horse after it was introduced by the Spanish, they didn't think of the horse as food (with the exception of the Apache).

The pioneers learned of jerky from the Native Americans, though most people on the frontier still seemed to prefer their meat fresh, salted down, or pickled. Jerky was used mainly by those with more of an Indian style of life, or those who were going to be away from civilization for some time: mountain men, hunters, and explorers. Since jerky wasn't commercially made, if you were going to pack any, you either had to make it yourself or buy it from Indians.

In the final analysis, dried meat (jerky) vs. meat preserved more-or-less whole was the result of the culture's food technology. The white man's farming and animal husbandry knowledge was better than the Indian's. Taken to its highest form, the white man's meat preservation skills have brought us SPAM. The Indian's gave us jerky. You decide which is best...

Incidentally, the Indians often took jerky, pounded it into powder, mixed it in a container with dried fruit, poured hot fat over it, and then allowed it to cool and solidify. Called "pemmican," white men who tried it weren't always enthusiastic about the taste, but it was said to be highly nutritious and could keep a person alive and well, especially in cold weather. Sort of a Native American "C" ration. In a later chapter I'll discuss pemmican at greater length for those who want to make some.

I don't know what led to the revival of jerky as a snack food in this country but one guess is the addition of flavoring. After slicing it into thin strips, the Indians generally just dried the meat out in the sun for three or four days. They did sometimes build a fire under the meat, mainly to provide smoke to keep the flies away. But beyond this, I have never read that they flavored it. (I have observed modern-day Eskimos in Alaska drying fish out in the open on racks. I didn't notice any fires, but that may be due to the scarcity of wood on the tundra.) Another factor is that when hiking and backpacking became popular, jerky became a convenient food to carry (like trail mix).

In any case, with the addition of different sauces and flavorings, today's jerky is not just an emergency or winter ration, as it was to the Indians, but a flavorful treat. Many people prefer it to the candy bars that often share shelf space with jerky in grocery stores, and it's far more healthful. But if you have bought jerky, especially in the smaller portions, you have probably paid around $1.25 to $2.00 per ounce. By using your oven and this book, you can bring your cost down to $.50 to $.75 an ounce. So, let's make jerky!

1.
The Tools

If making jerky is so simple, you may be wondering why you have to wade through this whole book. Jerky making is simple, but reading this thoroughly may save you from making a lot of false starts and less-than-perfect jerky. The first place to start is collecting the tools you'll need.

If you have a smoker—or a clothesline, for that matter—you could make jerky more-or-less in the old fashioned way. But it's faster and easier to use your kitchen oven, your biggest tool. Note that some ovens are hard to set below 200°F; their temperature settings start around 200° and don't really have a "warming" setting below that. If your oven will not allow itself to be regulated to 125° to 150°F, you have two choices: use the 200° setting and constantly turn your oven off and on while you monitor with a thermometer—a pain, at best—or find someone who does have a regulated oven and con him/her into making up the jerky.

Also take a look at your oven racks. The spacing of the grillwork will probably be too wide to spread meat out on the rack without the meat falling through to the bottom of the oven. To solve this problem, refer to Chapter 2 on the oven racks. In fact, before buying any meat or sauce, read through the whole book first.

The other items you'll need you should have around the house, unless you're like me, and get most of your meals out of a plastic pouch via the microwave. You'll need a glass or metal pan in which to marinate the meat. I use a 9" x 13" aluminum pan. I use two if I'm running different flavor bases. Then you'll need a smaller pan—say a 9" x 9"—to catch the drainings after you've soaked the meat. Large bowls also will work. Use a strainer or colander to catch the meat as you pour the marinade into the catch pan after soaking the meat.

For trimming the meat you should have a cutting board, a good sharp knife, and a fork (any kind, though I use a large meat fork) to move the meat around in the marinade sauce, or you can just use the point of the knife. I use a wooden cutting board, but one of the new synthetic material boards will probably work just as well. Use a knife that will take and keep an edge. You will need it to trim off fat on the edge of the slices, route out "junk" in the middle of the meat, and cut the slices to reasonable sizes if they are too big.

Two other items that are handy, but not essential, are an oven thermometer and a kitchen timer. The timer keeps you from having to be a clock-watcher. Set it for half way through the marinating time so you can move the meat around at least once. A thermometer comes in handy when you start, but after you've made a few batches, you'll probably know where to set the oven control. Just the same, it's a good way to check the temperature and it holds the oven door open about the right amount. Make sure you choose a thermometer that can register in the 100° to 150°F range and has a metal, not glass, shaft. Invariably, one day you're going to open the oven door and forget the darn thing is there and it's going to drop straight down. A metal one will survive; glass means you'll be picking up pieces.

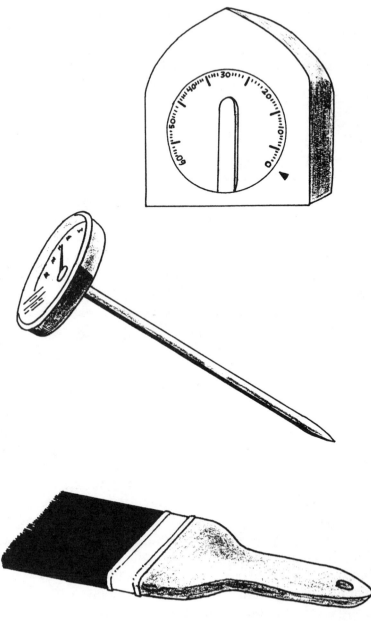

You can use a pastry brush to spread on any baste you want to add. But a paintbrush works best. They're also cheaper to use if you buy the bargain bundles at the discount store. One-half to one-and-a-half inches in width seems to work best. Just wash the brush well and dry after every use. Replace it if you start getting brush hairs stuck in your teeth when you eat the jerky.

I probably should mention here that there are various food dryers on the market. One type is shaped like a drum and consists of a heating element at the bottom and eight or more plastic trays that stack above it. They cost around $50. I bought one of these when I first started making jerky and they work just fine—for awhile. But then, as I started to dry large batches of meat, the plastic trays began to break, allowing the meat to drop through.

Another dryer, this time a square design with slide-out trays, was featured in a catalog I recently received. It came in three size and price ranges—from $130 to $220. It looked, from the picture in the ad, like it was also made of plastic, but since it said it was "dishwasher safe," I'm not sure. Certain plastics and heat, even from a dishwasher, don't go together too well. It looked like it would fit on a countertop, freeing up the oven for regular cooking.

I also have seen large, electric smoker-dryers made all of metal (aluminum and stainless steel). They are a bit clunky for kitchen use—the garage workbench would be a better place to put one—but they sure look durable and they could dry a heap of jerky at once. Again, they are a bit pricey for casual jerky making—around $150 to $250.

If you only plan to make occasional batches of jerky, a plastic unit will probably do. They are neat, easy to clean and don't take up much counter space or tie up the oven. But I wouldn't invest in one for heavy use unless it has a guarantee or is made of better material than the one I bought.

2.
The Oven Racks

Hopefully you haven't run out and bought all your meat, sauces, etc. before getting to this chapter, because if you did, you're in for a surprise! Your oven racks are too wide-spaced to hold the meat. You need something over the rack that will support the meat, allow air circulation, and withstand the heat. Also, it would be nice if you could use all four or five slots in your oven, rather than just one or two. (Most ovens come with just two racks.) After all, you pay for the same amount of gas/electricity no matter how many racks you use. So, how do we solve these problems?

DIRECTIONS FOR MAKING MORE OVEN RACKS:

Before following these directions, there are a few alternatives to making your own oven racks. You might try to buy new ones to fit your oven through the store where you purchased it or from a repair center that handles that brand. However, this could be fairly costly, if oven parts are anything like car parts. A second place where you might find oven racks is in the appliance scrap pile at your local dump. Poke around long enough, and you might find a few the right size. I imagine there's some sort of standardization in ovens. And if the local gentry happens by and sees you there, picking through

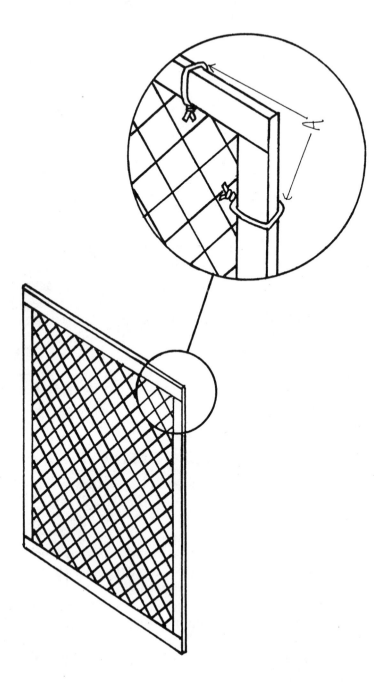

the garbage, you can just grin and say you dropped your watch and were looking for it.

But if these don't sound like good alternatives, you can make your own oven racks. That's what I did. Go to your building & supply store and buy a 48" x 48" screen door protector. These are framed pieces of fairly wide-meshed aluminum used to prevent damage to the lower half of the screen door, and they cost around $15 with an anodized bronze finish.

When you get it home look at the way the edging, which gives the mesh its support, is attached to the mesh. It should be slipped over all four sides and crimped down, with two of the edges overlapping the other two to provide more support. Using a screwdriver or other wide-bladed tool, pry up the edging just enough to slide it off all four edges of the mesh. Then cut two 16" x 20" sections out of the mesh. These two pieces, trimmed to fit your existing oven racks, will keep the meat from falling through.

The remaining mesh can be used to make two more oven racks. Measure the racks that came with your oven, and then cut out two sections of mesh to almost the same measurements, but make the width slightly narrower to accommodate the edging. Next, cut the edging to fit the four sides of each section of mesh. Make sure that one side of edging will overlap the adjoining edging to provide support. When finished, your new racks will look something like this (see facing page). Note the overlap detail in the exploded drawing of one corner.

After making sure that these new racks will fit your oven, hammer down the edging or crimp it with a pair of large pliers to secure it to the mesh. If it has a tendency to slip back off, loop some light wire (A) around the edging through the closest mesh, and twist it tight with pliers. Put a loop of wire at each end and in the middle on the long side. This should hold the edging well.

3.
The Meat

You can dry darn near any foodstuffs—fruit, veggies, etc. But I'm only into doing meat—beef, mainly. If you want to try other items, you can probably find information on them at your local health food store. Likewise, you can dry meats other than beef. I don't know how poultry would do—it's pretty dry meat to start with—but if you like your chicken the consistency of shredded wheat I guess it would work. Just the same, we will stick to beef in this tome. (If you drive the back county roads too fast at night, know a hunter, or like to do a little "moonlight grocery shopping," you may have access to venison. I would treat that the same as beef.)

What kind of beef should you use? Almost any cut will dry out, but not all make sense to use. Most cuts of beef, once dried, taste alike. Texture might vary, but all jerky tends to have a certain "chewiness" built in, so I doubt if you'd find it worth your while to use a tender filet mignon when a bottom round roast will do and is a lot cheaper. I mostly use bottom round or rump roast, though London Broil is about the best cut you can use if you can find it on sale. Bottom round can often be picked up for $1.69/lb. or less (1997). Other roasts that you'll often see on sale are tri-tip, cross-rib, and eye of round. All are good, but they may cost more and tend to have more "junk" to be trimmed out. But if they are on sale for less than rump, give them a shot. Just try to pick a piece of meat that looks "clean" (more on that below). Other cuts, London broil, flank, etc., make great jerky but are usually higher priced, the wrong shape, or shot through with fat and gristle. I'll expand on these three points.

HIGHER PRICED: This you can already figure. If most cuts of meat taste the same once made into jerky, you want to pick the cheapest cut that meets the other two requirements.

FAT AND GRISTLE: You'll want a piece of meat that isn't full of what I call "junk": fat, gristle, and other stuff. If you don't like having to spit out, chew around, or choke down all that non-meat stuff you often find in a roast, check both ends of the meat, trying to find the "cleanest" piece you can find in the counter display. This won't always assure you of a clean cut all the way through, as some rascally butchers can package the meat to look good on the ends but have half the cow's internal organs bunched in the middle. However, it's about all you have to go on.

You might be able to find an old fashioned butcher store, where they have the fresh meat displayed in a large case, not prepackaged into small plastic foam parcels. You can have the butcher hold the meat up so you can check out the ends and the general meatiness of the roast. What you want to avoid is excessive trimming, which takes time and leaves your meat pieces looking like doilies. It's really a joy when you get meat slices that only need to be cut in half and slapped into the sauce.

I usually find that a 3 to 4 lb. roast will give me a full oven-load of meat (using all four rack slots in my oven). About ¾ to 1 lb. of meat will fill a single oven rack. (How thick you have the slices cut will determine this.) If the butcher only has 10 lb. roasts, ask him to cut one down. Butchers will usually accommodate this request.

SHAPE OF THE MEAT: The main reason to use roasts is that you will need to have the meat sliced up (you can do it yourself if you have your own slicer), and you'll get a lot more usable meat off a big roast than most other cuts of meat. This is because the slicer has a tendency to screw up the first and last slice or two it cuts. The meat is uneven on the end and it takes one or two cuts to start getting even-sized slices.

Try to find a large roast that is "log shaped," longish with a good clear cross section on both ends of the log. Cut into its length, as shown, to give you the maximum number of large slices. Slicing against the grain seems to make the jerky tougher and doesn't make for as even a slice. (However, some people like it cut against the grain and you might want to try a cutting like this at least once to check it out.)

In the case of a roast that tapers down at the rear, cut into the wide front section and move back. You will get a little waste as you near the back, but this will still give you the best results. Bottom rounds and rump roasts are often cut for sale this way. If you have it sliced on its bottom, cutting up into the narrow "tip" of the roast, some of the slices will look like shoestrings. **Note:** The depiction of the knife in these last two illustrations (next page) is for clarity of method only. A butcher would use a circular slicer to make the actual cuts.

You sometimes see London Broil on sale, but it's usually cut into thick steaks instead of round roasts. London Broil makes nice jerky because it is generally fat and gristle free (there is very little waste) and it is a good cut of meat. If the price is right, pick the thickest "clean" one you can find, a steak 1" to 2" thick. Then have this steak cut in half. Now have the butcher slap

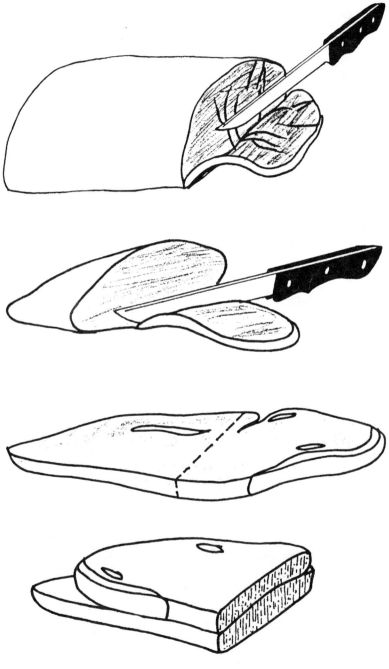

these two halves together. This will usually give the meat enough of a "roast" shape to slice well. He can slice it on end for long narrow strips, or on the bottom for big, wide slices. Works both ways. I prefer cutting it from the bottom. You get nice, big slices, even if you do lose a little section where the two halves meet.

If the only Broils available are already cut and wrapped and aren't very thick, you can still ask to have them cut in two, slapped together, and sliced, either on the broad side or on the edges. It will still work. Or you can ask the butcher to custom cut a thick piece the next time she is preparing meat for the display case, and you can pick it up when it's ready.

Also, prior to slicing any roast, ask the butcher to trim off all the outside fat. A good trimming will leave you less to have to do on your cutting board. If the trimmed-off parts are all fat, let the butcher keep them. If they contain a fair amount of meat, consider taking them home to your lawn decoration expert—Fido.

OTHER CONSIDERATIONS:

SLICES: How thick? This depends on your own tastes. My kids and I like thin, dry jerky. A lot of people prefer thicker, moister jerky, more or less similar to what you get over the counter at the 7-Eleven. Ounce for ounce there is more meat in a dry piece than a thicker, moister one, which contains more water. If you like the dry type, ask the butcher to cut the meat a little thinner than for lunch meat. Have her show you the third piece in, since the first couple of slices are often not true. You should be able to see light through it. If you want thicker, moister jerky, have the butcher slice it like thick bacon. Again, check the second or third slice in. In no case should it be thicker than the thick round slices of bologna you get in the prepackaged deli section. You can dry thicker pieces—I'll cover that later—but it really slows the process.

If you usually deal with only one butcher shop and the same slicer each time, you may learn just what slicer settings to use for a particular thickness. Be careful, though, because a number setting on one machine might give you a slice as thin as Kleenex, whereas the same number on another machine turns out slices like porterhouse steaks. The rolled roasts, such as cross rib, also tend to slice thinner for a particular slicer setting than the rumps and bottoms, which is not too important unless you are trying for thin, dry jerky. The slicer settings may vary as well over time and with repeated cleanings. To be sure, always check the third slice in.

Occasionally the slicer the butcher uses will give you one really big slab of meat. This generally happens near the end of the slicing, when the cowardly meat minion is reluctant to push down on the end of the roast and risk adding a few inches of finger to your jerky stash. If you can put a real sharp edge on the old meat knife you should be able to slice the slab down—be careful of your pinkies!—and get some slightly thick but dryable pieces out of it. If you can't, cut it into chunks and freeze them until you have enough for a good stew or shish kebab...or give them to Fido.

4.
Trimming the Meat

Because trimming is so important, both in saving you prep time in making the jerky and in getting full use of the meat you buy, I'm going to go on a little longer about it. Trimming can be the most time-consuming part of making jerky, other than drying time—and your oven does that for you. There are two kinds of meat market at which I usually shop. One is the supermarket type where the meat is already cut and wrapped and on display. If there is a butcher, and he's hidden in some back room, you can probably get his attention, and he'll trim and slice the meat for you.

The other type of meat market has an old-fashioned meat display case. Here the butcher stands behind a big counter in an apron, waiting for you to point out a choice of meat. She then cuts it to size, slices it if requested, weighs it, wraps the meat, and hands it to you. In the case of the supermarket, you can usually pick up the package and check out both ends and the top side of the meat. In the old-fashioned type market, you might only be able to see the top and one end, but on request the butcher will pull out a particular piece for your further inspection, so you can get a look at the entire roast.

In either case, the side that you can't initially see, the down side, will often have a layer of fat on it. This will vary, depending on the philosophy of the market, from a thin covering to a thick slab. In any case, you end up paying for this as part of the meat, but if the butcher removes it, you will save yourself a lot of trimming time.

The butcher I generally buy from knows just how I like my meat trimmed. Usually all I'll have is a very thin edging—or none at all—on the side of the meat that was so cleverly hidden in the store. This is often so light it can be left without further trimming, particularly with thin, dry strips of jerky. Other areas that might need trimming in your kitchen are small tips of gristle or hard fat on the end of the roast, and any marbling of fat that intrudes into the meat. This can come and go as you work through the slices. Large chunks of junk may also show up after you get into the center of the meat, but it, too, may disappear after half a dozen slices. This is the stuff you can't see in an outside inspection. You can get rid of it by "donut-holing" it (cutting it out) or you can section the slice into smaller pieces to cut around the junk. That is, slice the piece of meat in half, passing right by the junk. Then deftly cut out the junk with a "V" cut. These smaller slices will come in handy after you lay out the larger, whole slices because there will be open areas on the rack into which smaller pieces will fit nicely.

And speaking of meat layout, don't cover the rack so that it looks like a solid slab of meat. There needs to be some openings around the meat to allow the warm air to circulate. Also, really big slices are harder to store and take up a lot of rack room. Halving them allows more meat to fit into a given area without blocking air circulation. In any case, after you've run a few batches through, you'll see what I mean about well-trimmed meat saving you time and meat.

5.
The Sauce

Sauce is what separates just a piece of dried beef from a treat that once you start eating, it's like peanuts or popcorn. You start nibbling on it and before you know it, you've gone through enough slices to constitute a whole roast! Just wait until you take a big swallow of water. Bloat City!

The sauce or marinade is largely a matter of individual taste. I'm going to give you an overview of some variations that I use mostly when making jerky to order for friends, and the blend my family and I prefer. But the sky's the limit! Whatever you want to try may end up being just the ticket for you and yours. Anything that bombs out can be given to Fido...or taken to work and set out on a plate for your co-workers to consume.

I start most of my recipes from a soy sauce base, but not all. One friend likes what I call "nuclear" jerky. I soak it in Tabasco sauce, then drain it, and brush on a paste made from spicy-hot Kung Pao Sauce, chili powder, horse radish, cayenne pepper, curry powder—anything hot I can find. This stuff is best not consumed near an open flame.

A favorite with a lot of my friends is teriyaki flavor. I make a 50-50 mixture of soy sauce and red wine. To get the teriyaki flavor you can start with a teriyaki-flavored, soy-based sauce, or use straight soy and add a couple of packets of powdered teriyaki mix. You can also spread on a thick teriyaki baste or glaze (Kikkoman makes one) after marinating, when the slices are spread out on the racks. I often add a half cup of brown sugar to the batch to give it a sweeter flavor. Most people who eat my teriyaki-flavored jerky like this addition.

Besides the thick teriyaki baste brushed on after the marinade, mentioned above, there are many other sauces: sweet & sour is one, barbecue another. You brush all of these on after the meat has been drained and is lying on the rack. If you do add a baste or glaze, about half way through the drying cycle you may want to brush the surface of the meat so it will dry evenly, without any areas that don't dry properly because the glaze pooled.

If you make very big batches of jerky, you might want to buy soy sauce and baste in bulk at Price-Costco, Sam's, or similar stores. You will pay a much lower price buying in bulk than you will purchasing the small containers available at most supermarkets. Costco carries both teriyaki and plain soy sauce in gallon sizes, and sometimes soy sauce in 5 gallon jugs. (Before buying 5 gallons of soy sauce, however, make sure you will be making a lot of jerky. My last 5 gallon jug lasted almost half a year.)

I used to use a straight soy sauce marinade as my base but some people thought that the jerky was too salty, so I started cutting it with wine. I generally use a low-cost burgundy, but any popskull you have around the house will probably do. The alcohol gets cooked out in the drying so you don't have to worry about Aunt Minnie going out and picking fights in a biker's bar from chewing a few pieces. I have one friend who doesn't like the taste of soy and doesn't want wine used either. For him I don't marinate the meat at all, but just brush on a thick coat of teriyaki baste (glaze). Because I don't soak the beef in any other solution, I make sure it dries slowly and longer to prevent possible spoiling. I usually cut open a few sections to make sure it's dried all the way through before packaging it up.

My favorite flavor is what I call my "hearty-beef flavor" blend. This is a 50-50 soy sauce and red wine blend (about 24 oz. total), 6 to 8 oz. of Lee & Perrins Worcestershire sauce, and 4 to 6 oz. of A-1 Steak Sauce. Sometimes I'll add a little hickory smoke flavoring. I leave it at that, or sometimes brush on a barbecue sauce or salsa along with a sprinkling of black pepper. I'm sure that, with a little thought, you can come up with other blends and toppings. Just take care to write down what you use and the quantities; nothing can tick you off more than to hit on a sauce everyone raves about and then realize you don't remember the ingredients.

How long should you marinate? Different books I've read advise different times. The shortest I've run across says five minutes. One book suggested overnight, but most say 30 minutes. Since the meat only absorbs so much sauce, I use the 30-minutes guideline, giving the batch a stir at the 15 minute point. However, a longer time in the marinade might help tenderize a particularly tough cut of meat. In any case, I don't have a lot of patience and 30 minutes is what I use.

6.
Using the Oven

OK. We have the meat, it's been sliced, trimmed if necessary, soaked and drained, and is now ready for the oven. Take the drained meat and arrange it on an oven rack (see Chapter 2 about oven racks). You might put the rack over the sink to catch any drops still draining off while you're loading it. If you intend to add pepper, this is the time to sprinkle it on. Again, if you do a lot of jerky making, get the 1 lb. container from a discount food store

First turn the oven on to the "warm" setting. (Also, it doesn't hurt to line the oven bottom with aluminum foil to catch any drippings.) Most ovens have a warming setting, which might run between 125° to 175°. If your oven has a 150° setting, start there, or even lower. 125° to 140° will do the job, too. If the first marked setting is higher, about 175°, set it back about half-way to OFF, and put in the meat. Prop the oven door open about ¼" (maximum) and after the oven has been on for ten minutes, stick in your fingers. It should be quite warm but not uncomfortably so. Hot is out! You want to dry the meat, not cook it. Start filling the oven at the top rack slot. If you use all of your oven's slots, you may find that 150° is too hot for the lowest slot. Check the lowest rack (if used) after an hour of drying. If the meat there is getting hard or brittle, or looks like it's blackening, cut back on the heat or don't use the bottom rack.

Once you find a setting on the oven knob that always seems to give you the temperature you want, you might want to mark it with a felt-tipped pen or marker so you can go right to it each time. Then if you have a thermometer, you can use it just to monitor and fine-tune to one side of the mark or the other, depending on the drying requirements of the jerky you're making.

You can use the thermometer to prop the oven door open—the shaft is about the right size—by placing it in the center of the door opening with the shaft poking down into the oven interior. Then you can easily monitor the temperature. A thermometer isn't really necessary; I made jerky for over a year before I bought one, but a thermometer does make regulating easier, at least until you get used to your oven's settings. If you buy one, look on the kitchen utilities shelves for a thermometer with a metal shaft. A Cooper brand candy/deep fry thermometer is a good choice. It has dial markings that start at 100°F. There are several other brands on the market, so shop around. Prices of the metal ones range from $3.00 to $8.00, depending on the store. The main thing is to get one with a fairly low temperature reading and a metal shaft. Getting the drying temperature right is probably the trickiest part of the whole operation: too low, and it takes forever to dry the meat, too high, and you cook the bottom of the meat and leave the insides still pink, especially if you're drying on the bottom rack. (I've used 150° for a lot of jerky, though lately I've switched to 125° to 135°. It is an especially good setting for drying thicker pieces.)

If you're drying really thin jerky, you may be done in as little as four hours. Check the meat every two hours when drying thin sliced meat. If you're making thicker, moister jerky, it can take overnight (assuming you star⁺

around 6:00 PM) and you may want to cut the temperature down even more. The main problem in drying very
thin jerky is that there isn't a great deal of uniformity,
due to the slicer's inability to maintain consistency that
well with thin cuts. Because the meat won't be as even
as thicker cuts, you'll have to check it a little more often
and pull the very thin pieces out earlier than some of the
thicker thin slices.

With the thick, moist batches, you want to be sure
that you don't just dry, or even cook, the outside, leav-
ing the insides still pink and undried. With thick slices,
hold the temperature down until you get a feel for how
much heat is really necessary. If using all of the oven
racks, you might rotate them top-to-bottom at least one
time, too. Keep on hand a pair of those orange-handled,
stainless steel scissors that you can pick up for a couple
bucks in the grocery stores. If you're not sure whether a
piece of meat is done, use the scissors to cut through its
thickest part. When the complete interior is deep mahog-
any brown, the jerky is fully dried.

7.
The Procedure

I said making jerky is easy, but all this reading I've given you may make you wonder if jerky-making isn't right up there with discovering cold fusion. So, let me run through what it takes for me to knock off a batch (four oven racks) of jerky in an evening.

1. I stop off at the supermarket and pick out my roast, con the butcher into trimming and slicing it, and go on my way, trying to keep out of the bakery, which is always my waistline's downfall.

2. Around 6:00 PM I get out the pans and pour in the sauce, either starting with a new batch or using some I've had frozen or in the refrigerator. I trim the meat, if it needs it, and have my first batch soaking by 6:15. If I have two different flavors I'm marinading with, I might have two pans going. Each pan will handle about a pound of meat.

I set the timer to stir once at the 15 minute point. At 30 minutes it's time to pour the sauce and meat into a strainer, catching the juice in a smaller pan and transferring it back to the larger pan for the next batch. I use a fork to arrange the meat around the sides of the strainer to drain for a minute or two. If you have another batch of meat trimmed and ready, put it in the sauce in the large pan. Then put the drained meat on the rack, baste and season if you want, and into the oven with it!

3. I repeat until all four racks are filled (usually two batches). I should be done and have the pans cleaned up by 7:30. The pans and utensils can be washed up like anything else. The racks become crusty if not washed each time. I don't bother to clean them, because the residue gets hard and can be brushed off eventually. However, if you are the fastidious type, I suggest soaking them in hot soapy water for awhile and then using a scrub brush on them. Normally there's plenty of time between batches to feed the horse, have dinner, and resume your other usual activities. It isn't like you're slaving over the stuff all evening.

4. Once it's all in, check the batches around 10:00 PM (or about 2 to 3 hours later). The thinner sliced meat tends to stick to the rack, so pull each rack and move the pieces a bit. Doing this once is enough. Also, if any marinade has pooled, brush it out to ensure even drying. I always watch the 11:00 news, so I make a last check (and remove any done jerky) around 11:30. I usually have to get up once during the night to make a pit stop (approx. 3:00 AM) and I make a check then, too, removing any dried jerky. If you go to bed earlier and/or have a better bladder than I, just set the temperature down a bit when you hit the sack. After you've done a few batches, you'll have a better handle on where to set things. Each oven has its own peculiarities, but unless you have a really thick batch of meat, you should be able to remove all the jerky by morning.

8.
Storage

How long can you store jerky? Theoretically, jerky should last for months. The Plains Indians started drying buffalo meat as early as possible in spring and used that meat up until the time the big, shaggy animals showed up again the following year. Only, as I said earlier, I think the Indians dried their meat completely bone dry.

If you check the commercial jerky you buy in the store, it often carries a six month expiration date. That's pretty good, considering that the jerky is usually on the moist side. I think they get away with it because the sauce they soak the store-bought jerky in—call it embalmed—has a lot more nitrates and preservatives than the sauces I mention using. I've kept dry jerky in my refrigerator for up to a month without any problem, and if it is frozen, it should last indefinitely. But you'll probably find it isn't a problem keeping it fresh; it's a problem keeping it *around*! People tend to scarf the stuff up pretty readily. Still, if you aren't going to eat it right away, I suggest storing your jerky in the refrigerator, or if you have a really big batch, wrap it well and freeze it. This is particularly important with moister jerky if it is going to be around for awhile.

For how long is the sauce good? After a number of batches, juices from the meat will have leached out into the sauce. Despite all the salt and spices in the sauce, these juices will cause it to go bad eventually. I make it a habit never to use a batch of baste or marinade for more than three oven-loads. Also watch the color of the meat; it will usually look darkest when the sauce is fresh, and become lighter as you run through a roast or two. If the meat starts to look too light, that may be an indication that you should make a fresh batch of sauce or add a few more condiments to freshen the marinade.

If I won't be making all of my batches within one week, I freeze the sauce in between batches. Those are just my guidelines, but if there are any research-lab types out there who want to look into this with your batches of sauce, making up cultures of the marinade after a few runs, let me know and I'll update this book.

Speaking of freezing, you might be tempted to buy meat and have it sliced when you see it on sale. This isn't a bad idea, but I've run across a few pitfalls. If you are making mostly thin, dry jerky and you freeze freshly sliced meat for later drying, you may experience some loss of meat upon thawing. The thin slices tend to cling to each other and tear rather easily when you start preparing them after defrosting, so that you end up with a bunch of stringy shreds of meat instead of slices. Trimming the thicker slices while they're still half-frozen makes the job easier. If you're freezing sliced meat, my recommendation would be to freeze only the meat that's going to be used for thicker jerky pieces, not the ultra thin like I make for myself. If you do try freezing the thin slices, allow them to thaw *completely* before breaking apart the meat.

* * *

So that's it. Pick up some meat, some sauce, and see how easy it is. After a little experimentation, you should be able to make jerky as tasty as the jerky you buy at the store—better even. And I'm sure you'll save money over the commercial stuff. But you may find you're consuming more than ever as you become a jerky junkie!

If you have any problems/questions with making jerky at home, feel free to call me, Brad Prowse, at: (530) 273-8187. (But just don't call collect!)

9.
Pemmican

So one night you're in the kitchen, whipping up a batch of jerky—FAST! EASY! CHEAP! (We never give up on the PR work)—when you remember the name of another Frontier food: pemmican. You think, "Isn't pemmican an Indian food? Isn't it made from jerky? Couldn't I make that, too?"

Well, yes, yes, and yes—but you might not want to. Like jerky, pemmican was the Indians' backup food. But good as jerky is, man does not live by meat alone—there's also beer! Just kidding. Jerky alone is deficient in many ways. It is a good source of protein, but it lacks lots of the good stuff one gets from fruits, vegetables, nuts, and other foods. Pemmican was the closest thing the Indians had to a nutritionally balanced winter ration and it was used by many tribes, especially those who had to put up with hard, cold winters when game was scarce. Pemmican is a Cree Indian word, part of which means "fat," and, indeed, fat has a large part in the making of pemmican.

To make pemmican, the Indians started with long strips of jerky, made from deer, elk, buffalo, and so on. Once the meat was thoroughly dried in the sun and/or in smoke from a fire, it was pounded between two stones into a powder and then put into a leather pouch. Dried and ground-up fruits, such as wild berries and cherries, were mixed in with the powdered jerky. Next a good amount of melted fat and marrow was poured into the mixture and allowed to cool. Pastelike when cool, pemmican could be packed away and, if kept dry, would last a long time. Along with dried corn and other dried fruits and vegetables, it made up a large part of a tribe's winter rations.

Eating large quantities of fat may sound like less than gourmet-style dining, but in the bitter cold prairie winters it provided much needed calories. Still, it was apparently an acquired taste. Whites who tried it and reported the experience usually weren't ecstatic over it. But if there was no game, plants or fruit to eat, pemmican would sustain you until the warm months arrived. It's a little like having nothing but liver and onions and brussels sprouts to eat: You might not care for the taste, but it would keep you alive.

If you want to take a stab at making pemmican, about the only part that might be tricky would be the melted fat and marrow. You could use the oven to dry the meat and berries, but your local butcher would have to cooperate with you to get the fat and marrow. In the old days, when I was a kid, butcher shops tossed out the fat trimmings. Today, they collect the scraps in big barrels—probably to be sold to the fast-food hamburger joints—and you may have to pay for them. Obtaining the marrow might be more difficult, but since they have the beef bones there, I guess they could crack them for you— for a price.

After trimming the meat off the pieces of fat, you would have to render (melt) it in a large pot on the stove or in the oven. **Caution:** It's possible to overload your range exhaust fan and the hot fat is dangerous to move. It's about the same stuff they used to dump off castle walls on besiegers below—so be careful! I wouldn't pour the fat into leather pouches like the Indians did. Instead, you could mix the powdered jerky and berries in a bowl and then add the fat and marrow. After allowing the mixture to cool, wrap it, and store it in the refrigerator. If you make any, drop me a line and let me know how it went. BUT DON'T SEND ANY ALONG! If I feel a mid-winter craving for fat, meat, and berries, I'll hit that T-bone steak and Mrs. Smith's blackberry pie in the back of my freezer.

10.
Man-Afraid-Of-His-Horses

I have named my jerky making system Man-Afraid-Of-His-Horses, mainly because I feel the method is closer to the way the Plains Indians made jerky than is the commercial product now being sold. That is, it is usually more thoroughly dried and contains less additives and unnatural preservatives than jerky that must be able to stay on store shelves for months.

Man-Afraid-Of-His-Horses was a Sioux chief who, along with Red Cloud, refused to sign the treaty of 1866. This treaty, pushed by a peace commission headed up by the Indian Bureau, was to allow the Bozeman trail to pass through what was considered Sioux country and on into the goldfields of Montana Territory. Some Sioux chiefs, representing about 2,000 Indians, signed the treaty, but 4,000 other Sioux didn't go along with this intrusion into country they claimed for themselves. Ten years of warfare then ensued, culminating in 1876 on the banks of the river the Indians called Greasy Grass—known to us as the Little Bighorn River.

Man-Afraid-Of-His-Horses, by the way, was not afraid of his own horses. His name, as given here, was the white man's shortening of his actual Indian name, which went something more along these lines: "This is a warrior who is so feared that even the sight of his horses strikes terror into his enemies." In other words, other warriors, say the Sioux's traditional enemies, the Crow, were so in awe of this man's fighting prowess, that just the sight of one of his horses would frighten them...or the Sioux liked to think so anyway. The best the white man could do with a name like that was Man-Afraid-Of-His-Horses.

Your Jerky Recipes

Meet the Author

Brad Prowse is pictured here between his two horses, Zar and Jimmy. He was born in 1935 in Hayward, California, where his grandfather was a noted judge while the great uncles were "card sharks, gambling hall operators, and vigilantes." After serving in Korea in the U.S. Army, Brad returned to the U.S., married and became an electronic technician. His two children and four grandchildren live near his present home outside Grass Valley, California, where the author enjoys trail riding, collecting antique firearms, and spoiling his grandchildren. Mr. Prowse writes two monthly newspaper columns on Western history and home repair, and has also written a number of articles for horse and history magazines.